Cover Photo: English and Netherland Dwarf rabbits
Endpapers: Three young cross bred rabbits

HOWELL

Beginner's guide to

Rabbits

Will Bradford

Editor
Dennis Kelsey-Wood

HOWELL BOOK HOUSE Inc.
230 Park Avenue
New York, N.Y. 10169

Library of Congress Cataloging-in-Publication Data

Bradford, Will.
Howell beginner's guide to rabbits.

Summary: Discusses the basic aspects of caring for rabbits, including their feeding, breeding, exhibiting, first aid, and breeds.
1. rabbits–Juvenile literature. [1. Rabbits]
I. Kelsey-Wood, Dennis. II. Title.
SF453.2.B.73 1985 636′.9322 85-19769
ISBN 0-87605-943-4

Book design by Routedale Ltd, Liskeard, Cornwall, England
Printed in Hong Kong through Bookbuilders Ltd

Photographic credits:
© Panther Photographic International: pp. Cover, 10, 27, 31, 35, 39, 43 (top), & 50
© Diane Pearce: pp. 8, 24, 25, 32, 36, 37, 40, 41 & 49
© Sally Anne Thompson: Endpapers
© Paradise Press: All others and line illustrations

Contents

1. Introduction

The rabbit is a native of Europe, being found all over the continent and upon many of the offshore islands. It is abundant almost everywhere, except in the most northern regions. Curiously enough, the activities of man have probably been largely responsible for the spread of the animal. At the time of the Phoenician traders, about 1000 B.C., the rabbit was confined to the Spanish peninsula where it was common enough. Two factors apparently held it in check; these were the mountains across the narrow neck of land joining Spain and France, and the dense forests which formerly covered much of Europe. The ideal habitat for rabbits is grassland, interspersed with thin woodland.

Man unwittingly helped the rabbit to spread in two ways: by replacing forest by farm and pastureland, and by keeping rabbits for meat and for sport in special walled-in enclosures (leporaria) or upon islands. Some of these rabbit enclosures became quite famous and were visited by the aristocracy. No matter what precautions are taken it is difficult to prevent rabbits from escaping. They are tenacious burrowers, and swimming is not beyond their powers. Over the centuries, the rabbit population multiplied enormously, and largely at the expense of the hare, which was a direct competitor. The number of hares declined over the same period, although this may have

Family of Dutch rabbits

The 'racer' of the rabbit world – the Belgian Hare.

followed as much from the impact of man upon the environment as from the successful spread of the rabbit.

The rabbit is gregarious – colonies of them live in burrows underground known as warrens, banks and uncultivated ground being favorite sites. Under ideal conditions, these warrens may be surprisingly large and house scores of individuals. Rabbits tend to be crepuscular, emerging to feed at twilight and early dawn. Their diet consists of grasses and a wide variety of low-growing plants. The breeding season extends throughout the summer, the females producing as many as three or four litters, each of four to eight young. Young females may themselves start reproducing when they are only four months old. It is easy to imagine what potential there is for a population explosion! Fortunately, this is kept within bounds by overcrowding within the warrens and shortage of nearby food. In Great Britain, the rabbit population was greatly diminished by the outbreak of myxomatosis disease some decades ago, but the numbers are now again showing a steady increase.

The coat of the wild rabbit is a brown-gray color known as agouti. The stomach fur is light-colored or white. Weight may vary from 1·5 to 2·2 kg (3·3 to 4·8 lbs.), with a body length of between 22·9 to 29·2 cm. (9 to 11·5 in.). Some island races are smaller. The ears are large, erect and mobile, and the eyes are prominent. Although the body is compact, the hind legs are relatively large, compared with the front. This is mainly responsible for the characteristic hopping gait of the species, although rabbits can run very swiftly for short distances.

Domestication

The actual domestication of the rabbit, in the sense of confinement in hutches and controlled breeding, commenced about the Tenth Century A.D. Monks are said to have been among the first people to exploit the rabbit for meat and the practice was probably taken up by the peasants of the period. Although a nervous creature by nature, the animal was evidently adaptable to life in a hutch. The less nervous survived until the tame domestic animal of today was evolved. By the Seventeenth Century, rabbit breeding was common upon smallholdings, particularly in France and Germany.

Modern rabbit breeding may be said to have begun during the early and middle parts of the last century. About this time, the recognition of different breeds of rabbit began to take shape, based upon the colors and patterns which were then available. A distinctive color implied that the stock was domesticated and not merely confined wild animals. Besides, the colors were attractive and had novelty value. All of the older breeds of rabbit were established before the turn of the century, followed by the recognition of others during the early 1900s. Since then, few new breeds have been recognized, and today the emphasis is upon improvement of the many existing breeds.

Handling

A rabbit may be handled as easily as a baby: it is light and can be scooped up by sliding one hand under the stomach and lifting, or it may be cuddled with one hand on each side of the body. Young animals are inherently nervous and should be petted and fondled frequently. Shy individuals may need careful coaxing. Even half-grown animals should be given attention so that they become used to human beings. Such care and affection goes a long way towards producing friendly and responsive pets.

Adult rabbits are a different proposition. These should always be picked up with both hands. It is not correct to grasp the rabbit by a handful of hair and skin at the back of the neck, nor to pull on the ears – these are cruel practices. Experienced rabbit fanciers may be seen holding a rabbit by the ears with one hand, but this is what they are doing – holding the rabbit. Their other hand is taking the weight of the animal. Holding a rabbit in this manner is a knack, but one which is soon acquired. Any experienced fancier would be happy to demonstrate the method.

The majority of animals are tame and docile, especially if they have been handled from an early age, an elementary point, perhaps! However, there are two situations where some pugnaciousness may be displayed. A female may rise up in defense of her young, particularly during the first week or so after the birth. Any doe with a young litter should be treated with respect for a while. Presently, she will return to her usual friendly self.

Some males may become pugnacious when they reach full maturity. The reason is not obvious; it may be defense of territory, fearfulness if they have not been fondled sufficiently as youngsters, or they may have a need to assert themselves. It may also be an aspect of sexual rivalry, for bucks will fight each other viciously upon sight, whereas females are less prone to do so. Not all males will show signs of bad temper, indeed, one could say that they are in a minority. On balance, it is probably safer to choose a female if the rabbit is required solely as a pet.

Classification

The rabbit is a member of that advanced class of animals known as Mammalia: those which suckle their young and bestow considerable care upon their offspring. This group is sub-divided into many orders and the rabbit belongs in that called Lagomorpha. Lagomorphic animals bear resemblance to the great order Rodentia (mice and rats) but have different dentition (number and types of teeth). The lagomorphs have two incisor teeth, no canines, three premolars and three molars on each side of the upper jaw; and one incisor, no canines, two premolars and three molars on each side of the lower jaw. This is represented by the dental formula:

$$\frac{2\text{–}0\text{–}3\text{–}3}{1\text{–}0\text{–}2\text{–}3}$$

The rodents have only one incisor in the upper jaws and variable numbers of premolars (some have none at all).

The agouti coat color from which all present day colors and coat patterns have been developed.

The agouti color is seen in this Flemish Giant – of the standard British type. In the USA this variety may have numerous coat colors.

The Lagomorpha are divided into two families, the Ochotonidae (pikas) and Leporidae (hares and rabbits). The pikas are small animals about the size of guinea-pigs. Most species occur in Asia but two are known in North America. Hares and rabbits are far more numerous and wide-spread (some nine genera comprising fifty species) occurring throughout Eurasia and the Americas. Species were absent from Antarctica, areas of the Middle East, Madagascar and Oceanic Islands (Australia and New Zealand) until introduced by man.

The hare and North American rabbits (cotton-tails) are distinct from the European rabbit, differing in several fundamental biological details. For example, the hares do not burrow and their young are born, hidden in shallow 'hides', in a relatively advanced state, fully furred and with their eyes open. Cotton-tails have naked and blind babies, as do rabbits, but they do not burrow to any extent (unlike the rabbit).

The differences between the Old World or European rabbit, and its cousins, are recognized by placing it in a separate genus, *Oryctolagus*, containing only the single species *cuniculus,* and from which all present day domestic breeds have been developed. Therefore, *Oryctolagus cuniculus* is the scientific name by which the Old World rabbit is known world-wide, despite the many local names it enjoys in different languages and dialects. The species inhabits most of Europe which it populated in recent times from a restricted area of Spain.

The Classification of the Rabbit and its Near Relatives

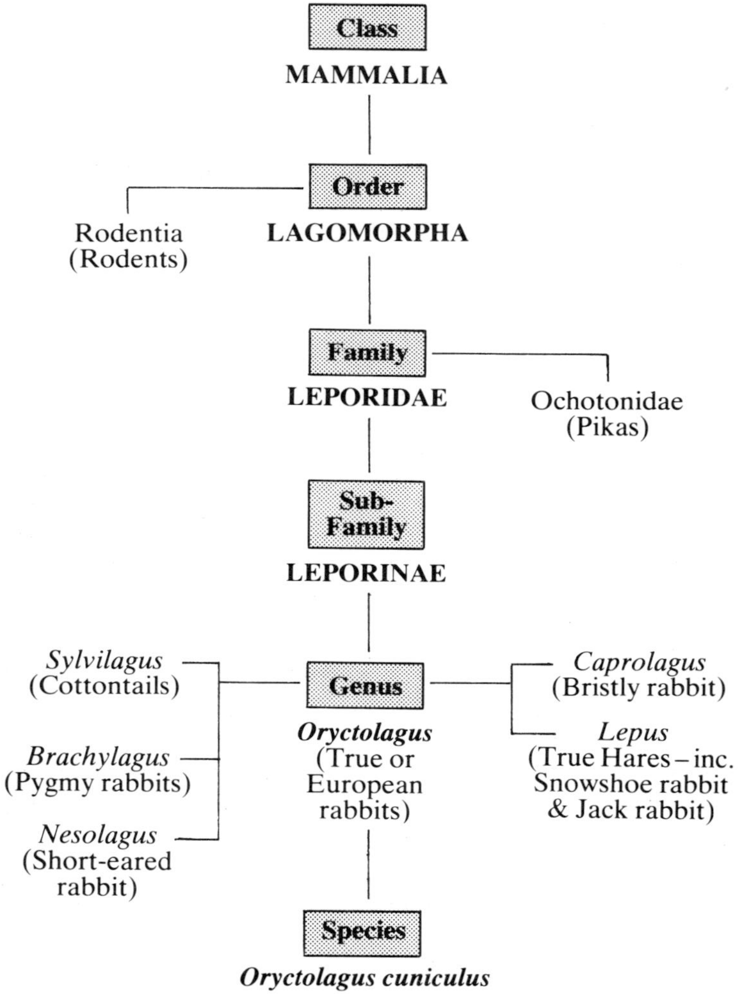

(All domestic rabbits breeds are developed varieties of this single true wild species)

2. Accommodation

The rabbit is a gregarious animal rather than a social one. Although, in the wild, warrens may comprise many individuals, each animal tends to keep to its own run. Attempts to keep two or more adult rabbits in the same hutch will sooner or later end with serious injury. Each rabbit must be housed in a separate hutch.

Hutches

Rabbit hutches are conventionally constructed of wood, rectangular in shape, and either partially, or completely, open-fronted. The size may vary with the breed of rabbit; the larger the breed, the greater the required floor space. A medium-sized breed would require a hutch of the following approximate dimensions: 40cm. (16in.) high, 40cm. (16in.) deep and 100cm. (39in.) long. The hutch itself may, or may not, be divided into two sections: a small compartment for sleeping and nesting, and a larger one for living. Two doors may be fitted: a solid door for the smaller compartment and a wooden frame door for the larger. The wood frame should be covered on the inside with 1·3cm. (0·5in.) heavy-gauge wire-netting. Alternatively, use similar size weld-mesh netting. A removable thin board, about 7–10cm. (3–4in.) high, should be slotted just inside the door to prevent the inmates from overbalancing, whenever the door is opened.

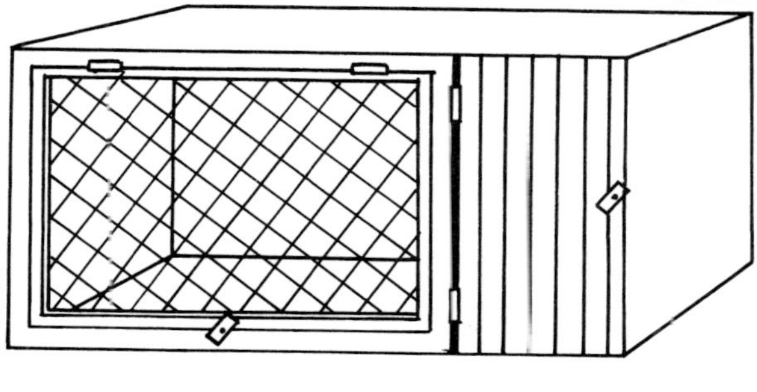

A typical Indoor Hutch

Many hutches are made with a single, large, wire-meshed door; that is, the sleeping compartment has been dispensed with, allowing more room for exercise. These hutches are ideal for bucks. For does, the nesting compartment is replaced by a 'nest-box'. This is a solid box, measuring about 25cm. (10in.) high, 25cm. (10in.) wide and 40cm. (16in.) long, open at one long side, except for a strip of wood about 7cm. (3in.) along the bottom. This strip holds the nest materials together and the doe soon learns to use the box for dozing as well as nesting.

Most doors are constructed to hinge on one side, but this is not always so, nor are these necessarily the best. Some hutch doors may have hinges at the top so that they can be propped open, while others may have hinges at the bottom so that the door can fold down. Still others sport a door which lifts completely out of the way. All of these designs are meant to ease the routine of feeding and cleaning. No obstructions should be put in the way of rapid cleaning.

The walls and floor of the hutch should be made of close-fitting boards, so as to exclude drafts and to avoid cracks which may catch the rabbit's claws. The interior of the hutch should receive two to three coats of paint, light-colored, for preference, so that the animals can be readily seen. Always choose lead-free paint. The floor should be covered with a layer of sawdust to absorb urine. Wood shavings may be used, but they are less suitable.

A battery of nine hutches. Note the roof overhang and the clear space beneath the hutches.

Bedding may be of straw or hay, the latter serving also as an important constituent of the diet. In fact, ample hay should always be freely provided.

The hutches should be inspected for cleaning about once per week. All dirty sawdust, droppings and damp hay should be removed. Most rabbits habitually excrete in one particular corner of the hutch and this usually facilitates cleaning. A small shovel, or scraper, is the appropriate tool to use for this purpose. It is often convenient to remove the rabbit temporarily during cleaning out, since some animals become upset, and claw at the utensils. They are obviously disturbed by the intrusion of strange objects into their home.

Rabbits may be kept either outdoors or indoors. Outdoor hutches must be robust and constructed to preclude drafts. The animal is very hardy and can tolerate quite cold conditions, provided it is not exposed to drafts or damp. It is advisable to cover the outside of the hutches with roofing felt. It is useful to have a roof which extends beyond the front of the hutch; not only will the hutch be protected, but so will the person attending the stock. Outside hutches are normally arranged in stacks of about three high. It is inadvisable to have the first too close to the ground and the top-most hutch must be easy to reach. However, the arrangement of hutches will depend upon the space available and how many rabbits you intend to keep. Consider erecting the hutches in the lee of a building or a wall.

It is more pleasant, both for the rabbits and for their owner, if the hutches

Rabbits, and guinea pigs, are seen at their best if given the room to exercise

are indoors, in a shed or an unused garage. However, it is advisable for the shed to be well-ventilated and not too dark as rabbits suffer in very hot, stuffy conditions. Open windows should be covered with wire-netting tacked onto the inside to keep out intruders. One advantage of a shed is that it can be illuminated with electric light, thus enabling stock to be attended after dark – which is a boon on wintry evenings. If artificial heat is installed, it needs to be minimal, just sufficient to keep the temperature above freezing point. This amount of warmth is sufficient and will also prevent the green food from freezing in the hutches. Of course you can increase the warmth for your own comfort if you wish.

Hay Rack

Hay may be simply placed on the floor or pushed into so-called 'hay-racks'. These may be made from wire mesh and stretched across the angle between the wall and the ceiling of the hutch. Use a wide mesh so that the rabbit can easily pull the hay through. The end of the rack facing the door is left open so that the hay can be quickly inserted. The use of racks is hygienic and prevents the hay from becoming fouled by damp sawdust.

Bowls and Water Bottles

Essential accessories to the hutches are few. Corn mixes or mashes should be given in feeding bowls. These should be made of heavy material, such as glazed earthenware, otherwise the rabbit will almost certainly tip them over, wasting valuable food. If water is given in bowls, these can become soiled with dirty sawdust. A better method of providing water is by using a water

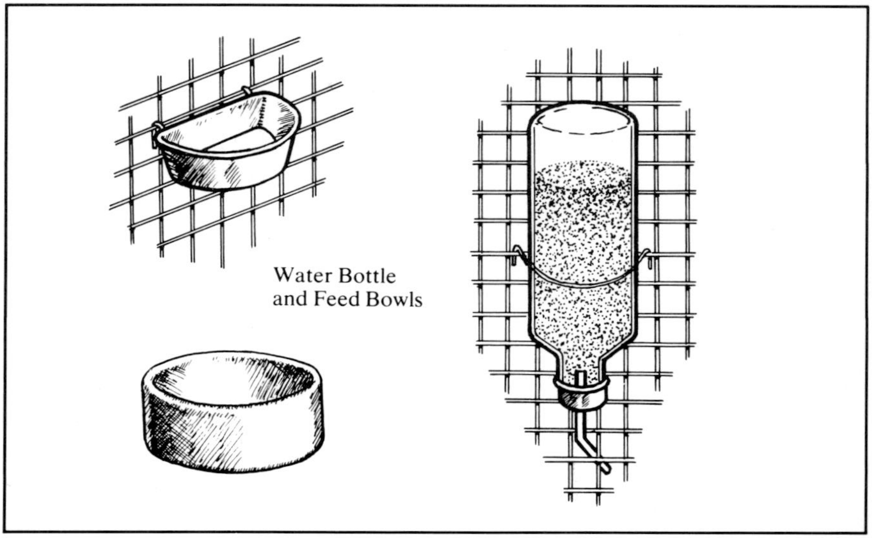

Water Bottle
and Feed Bowls

bottle. There are special bottles on the market fitted with a bung and a pipette for the rabbit to suck. The bottle is commonly hung on the outside of the wire door, with the pipette bent so that it intrudes through the mesh at a point where the rabbit can easily reach it. The bottle may be refilled as required. Be careful not to allow green algae to collect on the inside of the glass. This may be cleaned off by dropping some fine sand into the bottle with a little water and vigorously shaking it.

Morant Pens

Light outdoor pens may be used in which the rabbits can have a playful romp in the sun or in which young stock can be reared to maturity after weaning. These pens are known as Morants and are light frame-works of wood covered by wire mesh. They are commonly triangular in shape and of a convenient size for moving. Handles may be fitted at each end for ease of transport. A portion of the pen should be covered to afford shelter in the event of storms. These pens are useful for putting the rabbits out to graze, the wire mesh on the base being as large as 5 to 8 cm. (2 to 3 in.) to allow the stock access to the grass. The pens must be moved frequently so that the grass is not damaged by over-grazing or the accumulation of urine. The young rabbits will not thrive on grass alone but must have the usual cereal mix and plenty of hay.

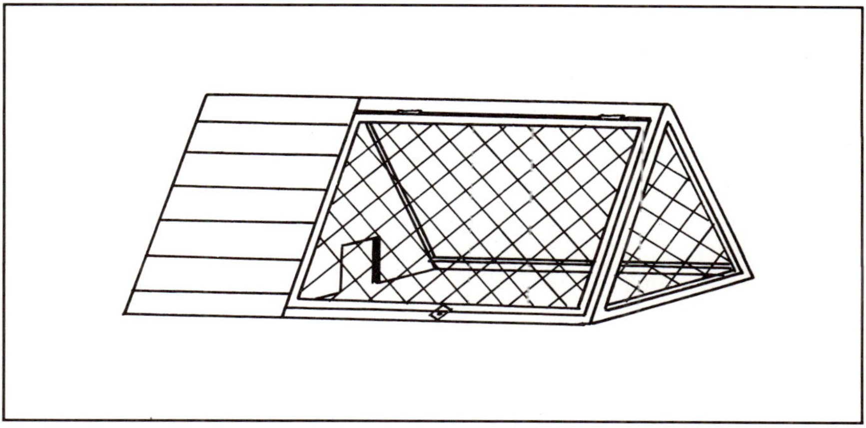

Rabbit Manure

Rabbit cleanings are a valuable manure, as any knowledgeable gardener can tell you. By rights, they should not be thrown into the refuse bag, but placed on the compost heap. The sawdust and droppings will rot down quickly if mixed with compost materials. This aspect of rabbit-keeping should not be overlooked by those people interested in the use of 'natural' methods of gardening.

3. Feeding

The rabbit is a simple animal to feed, not requiring the expensive diet, for example, that must be provided for a cat or dog. In point of fact, if one is careful, the scraps from one's table or waste from the kitchen garden can supply the bulk of the necessary food. The dietary requirements for the rabbit can be grouped under four headings; cereals or corn, green-food, root vegetables and hay. These are discussed in turn.

Cereals

Cereals are corn mixtures of various compositions. These are the most concentrated food a rabbit receives and should be fed in such quantity that scarcely any remains by the next meal. The most popular cereal is oats, whole or crushed, followed by bran; but wheat, barley and maize can also be given. It is convenient to feed mixtures of cereals, rather than a meal consisting of all of one sort or a number of separate items. One can buy rabbit mixtures from pet stores, or you might want to try making up your

The Californian rabbit was bred for its fur and meat. However, it makes a fine pet – the Himalayan markings being most attractive.

The long pendulous ears of the Lop rabbit will need constant care.

own. Oats and bran should be the basis of most mixes, but with additions of wheat, barley and maize. Use flaked maize rather than crushed maize because it is more nutritious. Various mixes should be made in order to find which the rabbits like best.

Whichever mixture is decided upon can be fed dry or damped to a crumbly state by adding water. Indeed, many fanciers add milk to the corn mix for pregnant and suckling does. Such preparations are known as 'mashes' and are more palatable than dry feeds. Both dry and mash mixtures should be given in small bowls or feeding pots, preferably of a heavy, earthenware nature to prevent them from being easily overturned. Many rabbits take a fiendish delight in overturning feeding bowls, spilling and wasting the contents. Dry mixes can be made in quantity and fed as desired, but mashes must be made up daily. A traditional mash is boiled potatoes dried off with bran and is a diet which most rabbits will accept eagerly. Always discard any mashes left uneaten.

Cereal scraps from the table are relished by the rabbit. Such items as cookies (biscuits), cake, bread crusts or similar, should not be thrown away but put aside for the animal. Stale bread, in particular, is most useful. If baked dry in an oven as cubes or rusks, it will not only keep as a stand-by food, but it will give the rabbit something hard to gnaw. This will keep the animal occupied and is good for its teeth.

Special rabbit pellets may be purchased from most pet stores. These have been specially developed for the species and contain, in addition to concentrates, grass meal to represent green-food. Theoretically, these constitute a complete diet when fed in conjunction with hay and water. It must be admitted that pellet feeding can save a great deal of time – a not inconsiderable factor nowadays. Against this, is the fact that rabbit pellets are relatively expensive. They should thus be viewed as a valuable stand-by in the event of a sudden shortage of cereals or green-food. There is no reason why a few pellets should not be added to the corn mix, if only to ensure that the stock are used to them.

Green-food

The rabbit is fundamentally a herbivore; that is, its staple diet is green-food which, in its natural state, it consumes in large quantities. This food can consist of young blades of grass, leaves and shoots of many plants, even small branches of shrubs and bark. Hutch-bred rabbits have been fed on kitchen waste from time immemorial. Unwanted leaves of cabbage, cauliflower, greens and lettuce may be fed, as well as apple and potato peelings, tops of carrots, celery and radish, pea-pods and the like. Trimmings from a greengrocer or food store can often be had for the asking or for a few cents.

People who are lucky enough to have a kitchen garden will have little problem in keeping a small number of rabbits. The normal wastage from vegetable crops can be used to good effect. Nevertheless, it may be wise to plant a few extra items specially for the rabbits; a few extra cabbages or Brussels sprouts, for example, or a quick-growing vegetable like lettuce. Root crops to form a winter reserve of food are also an excellent idea. If a large number of rabbits is kept, growing your own green food will save you a lot of money.

Wild green-food should not be overlooked, especially if it can be obtained simply for the gathering. Any of the following may be fed to rabbits: dandelions, clover, dead nettles, chickweed, groundsel, dock, plantain, shepherds purse, thistles, vetch, yarrow and colts-foot. Leaves are more nutritious than stems, particularly old stems, so endeavour to collect new growth where possible. Young grass can be clipped with shears and included in the mixture. No green-food should be gathered from areas which have been fouled by dogs or subjected to automotive exhaust fumes. This may not be easy to avoid but the risk is that of disease or poison.

Unfortunately, there are a number of wild plants which can be injurious. These are any plant with a bulb, bindweed, buttercups, ragwort, foxglove, scarlet pimpernel, speedwell, charlock, elder, toadflax, nightshade and hemlock. It is useful to have an illustrated book on wild plants to identify those which can be safely fed and those which cannot. It is wise to take the attitude 'if in doubt, leave it out' to be on the side of safety. Follow the principle of feeding a variety at all times and, if any particular plant is habitually left uneaten, omit it in the future. A well-fed rabbit will usually refuse harmful plants.

Root Vegetables

Several varieties of roots may be fed, especially in winter when green-food may be relatively expensive or even unobtainable. Roots comprise carrots, swedes, turnips, parsnips, beetroot and the many other comparable vegetables. All of these are nutritious and can be given at any time in addition to the usual leafy green-food. They can, of course, be either grown or bought as required. The rule to follow is not feed too much of any one item, but to provide a mixture. Rinse and dry all roots if these are dirty. Small potatoes, usually rejected for consumption, may be given provided these are not green. They may also be cooked and fed as the main constituent of a mash.

Hay

The provision of good-quality meadow hay is essential. It is nutritious to some extent, but its main function is to furnish bulk. An ample supply should always be available. It can be tossed into the hutch or pushed into wire racks fixed to the wall of the hutch. The hay should be clean and smell fragrant. There should be no signs of mold nor should it smell musty.

Straw can be given in addition to hay but not as a substitute. Judging by eating habits, rabbits do not like straw as much as hay. Straw should be looked upon as a useful bedding material.

Water

Many oldfashioned fanciers insist that water is unnecessary for rabbits. Well, it is, up to a point, if ample green-food is available. However, the modern view is that the provision of water is desirable. The stock will certainly drink if they have access to water. Water may be given in heavy bowls or in the form of a water bottle. The latter can be fixed to the outside of the hutch with a drinking spout protruding into the interior. If rabbit pellets are fed, water is a must.

How Often to Feed

Rabbits like a settled life and should be fed at roughly the same time each day. They may be fed once daily, but twice is to be recommended. This

A Silver Rex rabbit. The short plush coat is available in many colors and other varieties of rabbits may also have Rex coats.

should be in the early morning and again in the early evening. These times accord with the rhythm of feeding of the wild animal. For instance, cereals and some hay could constitute the morning feed, followed by green-food and additional hay in the evening. In hot climates 'mash' feeds are best given in the evening thus less likely to sour in strong sunlight and high temperature.

As to quantities, be guided by the amount consumed between meals. Sufficient should be given so that just a little is left uneaten between feeds. Small breeds will eat less than large ones. A doe mothering a litter will require more than a doe by herself. Also, when the litter is old enough to take solid food, one must be prepared for the quantity to increase almost daily. Be very careful in the hygienic handling of food, for young rabbits are very vulnerable to stomach upsets. Ensure that the green-food is fresh and the hay has a pleasant smell.

4. Breeding

The breeding of rabbits presents no special difficulties but is a little more complex than, say, that of mice. With mice, a pair (male and female) may be placed in a cage and left to their own devices. Since rabbits have to be housed in separate hutches, this is impossible. A different approach must be employed, that is all, for rabbits breed prolifically. In rabbit-breeding circles, the male is known as a 'buck' and the female as a 'doe'.

Mating

Sexual maturity or puberty, will vary with the breed. Small breeds mature more quickly than large ones, frequently at the early age of four months, while the very large animal may not be ready until it is seven months old. The average age, however, is around six months for both sexes. A vigorous buck will show a persistent interest in does and be ready to mate at any time. On the other hand, the doe may or may not be ready to accept a buck upon a particular day. The two sexes have to be placed together and the mating supervized.

The Angora rabbit is the opposite of the Rex for it sports a long soft woollen coat

It is usual to introduce the doe into the hutch of the buck. If the doe is not ready for mating, she will probably give the buck a cold shoulder or even snap at him. If the latter happens, quickly remove the doe before any serious damage can be inflicted. A reluctant doe should be tried as frequently as necessary, on a daily basis, until she eventually accepts the buck.

When a doe is ready for mating, she will crouch on her stomach and allow the buck to mount her. A successful mating is usually signalled by the buck giving a convulsive lurch and falling off the doe. It is advisable to permit several acts of mating before the doe is removed to her own hutch. An eager buck may fuss over a doe for several minutes before a successful mating is accomplished. This is particularly true for inexperienced bucks, so be patient.

The domestic rabbit will breed at any time of the year, although the natural period is the spring and summer. This is the best time for breeding. Three or more litters can be bred each year. If the animals are merely kept for pets, an occasional litter from time to time adds to the joy. However, if you are breeding for exhibition, the matings have to be carefully planned. Serious fanciers arrange the matings so that the young are maturing and at their best at the right time for the major events of the show season.

Litters

The doe carries her young (gestation period) for an average of thirty-one days. The impending birth of young is heralded by the doe building a nest of hay or straw, either in one corner of the hutch or in a nesting box – if this is available. The doe will pull fur from her chest and stomach to line the nest. It

The beautiful Himalayan rabbit. Its dark points – nose, ears, feet and tail are characteristic of this variety and its name is used to describe this color pattern in other varieties.

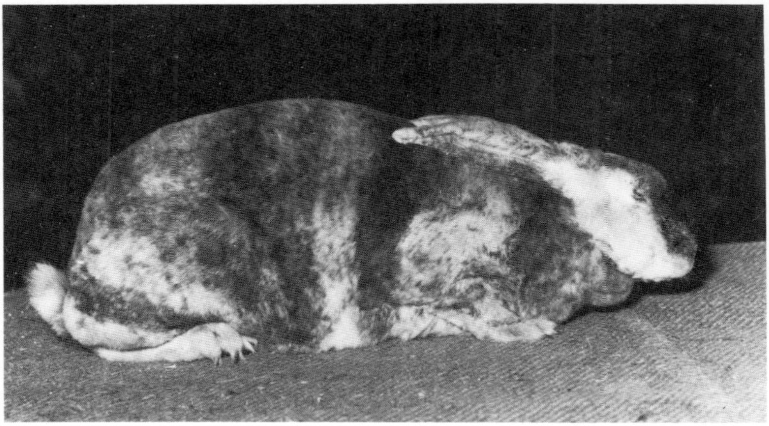

The Harlequin rabbit – quite rare and very much for the specialist.

is most unwise to touch or interfere with the mother, or young, at this stage for at least ten to fourteen days, otherwise she may turn on her babies. As soon as the young start to venture from the nest, both the doe and her litter can usually be fussed over without fear of the consequences.

Baby rabbits are born naked with closed eyes, and a litter may number from three to eight. The average is about five or six; small breeds having less, while large breeds frequently have many more. By about ten days, the young have grown fur and their eyes are beginning to open. Very soon, they will leave the nest for short periods to forage for food. The mother will suckle the litter until the young are about five to six weeks old when it is time to think of weaning them. It is not advisable to leave the young too long with their mother because of a slight risk that she will savage them.

It is common practice to give the young saucers of milk or such things as bread soaked in milk. This is not really necessary although it may add to the fun of rearing a litter. Often the mother may quaff the milk before the babies have had a chance to drink. Mashes made with milk instead of water are a common practice and have advantages over saucers of milk. Young rabbits require water and if a water bottle is used, make sure that the nozzle is low enough for them to reach it easily.

It is uncommon for a doe to commence building a nest sooner than a few days or a week before the birth of a litter. Fur may even be plucked from the body. However, if a doe does so about the sixteenth day of gestation, this is a sign of a mis-mating, an event which fanciers know as a 'phantom pregnancy'. The doe should immediately be tried with a male for in this condition she will often readily accept a mating. None-the-less, there is a chance that the pregnancy may be real, so promptly remove the doe from the buck's hutch if she should resist him.

The strain of rearing a litter may easily cause a doe to lose some of her fine condition. This is normal and she should regain her usual good health once the litter has been weaned. Further litters from the doe should be delayed until she is back in full condition. However, watch that she does not become too fat, otherwise she may persistently refuse to mate. A green-food and hay only diet is the cure for such recalcitrant animals.

Sometimes a doe may lose or neglect her litter due to a mishap. Young does with first litters are most prone to such accidents. The loss of a litter is usually due to a strange or exceptionally loud noise disturbing the doe at a critical time. It is wise to attempt to mate the doe quickly, the same evening, if possible. The reason is that most does will accept mating immediately after littering and prompt remating will help to disperse the milk. Milk will be forming in the milk glands of the doe in order to feed her babies. Since there are no babies to suckle, milk can accumulate in the glands which can become congested, hard and tender, a disorder known as 'milk fever'.

Sexing

A litter of young may be kept together for about three months, rarely longer, otherwise fighting may break out or, worse, litters may be born to immature does. It is good policy to divide the litter, by sex, at an early age. Sexing is not difficult in animals of six weeks or older. The vent should be examined and the skin peeled back. If a small tube slowly emerges from the skin fold, the individual is a male; if a slit is evident, the individual is a female. It is not long before the tube or penis is so large that the sex is unmistakable. Just before or upon reaching puberty, the testes descend into two pinkish sacs on each side of the penis. On average, the litters will consist of half males and half females.

Fostering

Fostering is the act of moving babies from one nest to another. The reason for doing this is that a doe with a small number of young in a litter can relieve the strain imposed upon one with a large number. It is a delicate operation for does know their own babies by sense of smell and will kill strangers. Experienced fanciers will have the skill to foster babies between litters but beginners should not attempt it. Does can quickly take offense if their young babies are touched and will destroy the whole litter if unduly provoked.

A beautiful study of the satin chocolate Tan rabbit.

5. Breeds

Rabbits may be purchased from most pet stores. These are rarely other than cross-breeds or mongrels, although occasionally a few animals of recognized breeds may be found. Cross-bred rabbits should not be overlooked for they can make fine pets. The advantage of them is that they are usually hardy and inexpensive to buy. Once experience is gained, one can then move on to better quality animals. There are enough breeds and varieties to satisfy even the most demanding purchaser.

The best method of deciding which breed has the greatest appeal is to visit an exhibition. Specimens of most breeds will be on view and these can be compared. Also, contact will be made with specialist breeders who will be happy to discuss the merits of various breeds. The wild rabbit is an agouti gray but breeds exist in many fascinating colors. These have arisen in the past as mutations, or 'sports', and have been retained by breeders because of their novelty and attractive appearance.

Rabbits are recognized, both as breeds and varieties, and it is useful to be aware of the distinction. Breeds are defined by size and conformation, the latter term meaning the shape of the animal – whether it is short or stocky in build, for example, or long and slim, or any body shape in between. On the other hand, a breed may exist in many colors and these are known as varieties. Therefore, the breed designation has first priority, with variety as a secondary consideration.

There are two broad categories of breeds. These are fancy and fur. The fancy breeds are those bred mainly for show purposes whereas the fur breeds are bred for more general purposes. It is the older breeds which come into the fancy category, while the more modern breeds were evolved for their fur. With fur breeds, the greater emphasis is placed on coat quality rather than in the exact position of pattern.

Fancy Breeds

Angora

This is the long-haired rabbit. It is of medium size, about 3·2kg. (7lbs.) in weight and characterized by long, silky-textured, hair. Exhibition animals require constant attention, combing and grooming, to prevent the fine hair

The very popular Dutch rabbit seen in profile.

Head study to show the facial stripe – somewhat wide in this example.

from matting, while the hutches must be kept spotlessly clean. Thus, unless you are prepared to spend time on your charges, this may not be the ideal breed to keep. Animals not kept for showing or breeding stock may have their coats clipped short. This does not harm the individual and avoids the nuisance of unsightly matting.

Belgian Hare
A breed which looks similar to the wild hare. The animal is bright in color ('rich chestnut') and is long and 'racy' in appearance. Very popular at the turn of the century it is now less common. Needs plenty of exercise to keep in fit, hard condition. Weight guide 4·1 kg. (9 lbs.).

Dutch
One of the most popular breeds, it is a small rabbit weighing about 2 kg. (4·5 lbs.). The head is divided by a narrowing stripe of white extending from the nose to between the eyes; the fore part of the body is white, while the

hind part is colored. The colored parts may be black, blue, chocolate, brown-gray, steel-gray, tortoise-shell or yellow. In practice, it is difficult to obtain the exact pattern required by the exhibition standard for the breed.

English

The second of the popular 'patterned' breeds, it weighs around 3·2kg. (7lbs.). The animal is white, except for spots of pigment on the face and body. There must also be a 'herringbone' of pigment down the spine. In the ideal English, the spots must occur in the right places and be of the correct size – a very difficult proposition! The colored spots may be black, blue, chocolate, tortoise-shell or gray. Either the Dutch or English would present a real challenge to any breeder who is interested in breeding them.

Flemish Giant

One of the largest breeds in existence. The bucks may scale over 5kg. (12lbs.) and the does are even heavier. In Britain, only the steel-gray is recognized but, in the U.S.A., the Flemish is known in several colors. In fact, although it is as large as the English version, the U.S. Flemish is a somewhat different breed. It will need spacious accommodation and has a large appetite, both of which the beginner should consider before purchasing this breed.

The English rabbit is always seen in good numbers at rabbit shows and is deservedly a popular pet.

English and Netherland Dwarf (Smoke Pearl color) rabbits.

Dwarf rabbits are available in most colors – here we see the Himalayan variety.

Harlequin
The 'soccer jersey' rabbit, for the coat is a pattern of black and yellow stripes. It is also possible to have chocolate and yellow or blue and cream. The Magpie is the same as the Harlequin except that the yellow stripes are replaced by white ones – rather uncommon as a breed, but most intriguing.

Himalayan
The Himalayan is medium-sized, about 2·3 kg. (5 lbs.) and is white except for the nose, ears, feet and tail (the 'points', as fanciers say). The points may be any one of the four colors: black, blue, chocolate or lilac.

The Netherland Dwarf was developed in Holland – compare this white one with its alternative below. Note its head and ear shape and length.

A white Polish Dwarf rabbit. Although ideal as pets, Dwarf rabbits can be difficult to breed and are not recommended for beginners who plan such.

Lop
The breed with the enormously large ears. These are bred in several colors since it is the size of the ears which counts. Not a rabbit for the novice, for the ears must be kept in tip-top condition and not allowed to become damaged in any way. They will weigh an average of 4·1kg. (9lbs.).

Netherland Dwarf
The first of the two very small breeds – it weighs about 0·9kg. (2lbs.). It is deservedly popular, because it is easy to feed and house, and because of the many colors of which it boasts. In fact, almost all of the known colors in rabbits may be found in the one breed. This is very much the breed for the experiment-minded hobbyist.

Polish
A worthy companion to the Netherland Dwarf. It is very petite and lively in behavior. Bred in as many colors as the Netherland, it often rivals it in popularity. The weight of this small breed is in the region of 1kg. (2 to 2·5lbs.).

Silver
A medium-sized breed uniquely covered in a liberal sprinkling of white hairs (the 'silvering'). The ground color may be black, brown-gray or fawn.

Tan
A compactly built animal with yellowish-tan stomach fur. The coat on the back may be black, blue, chocolate or lilac. The stomach fur color is lighter in the blue and lilac than in the black and chocolate.

Fur Breeds

Alaska
A self-colored black animal, the color being as solid and glossy as possible.

Argenté
A heavily 'silvered' breed. The silvering is so profuse that the rabbit seems white with colored flecking. There is the Argenté *champagne* (with black flecking), *bleu* (with blue flecking), *brun* (with brown flecking) and *crême* (with fawn flecking): The Argenté is born self-colored, with the white overlay appearing in later molts. Weight varies according to color in the range 2·3 to 2·7kg. (5 to 6lbs.).

Beveren
One of the original fur and meat breeds and still very popular, it will weigh about 3·2kg. (7·5lbs.). The white has a dazzling white coat and blue eyes, while the blue has a light blue coat. There are also the black and the brown, but these are less frequently seen.

Californian
A large rabbit developed in the U.S.A. for meat and fur production. The body fur is white but with colored extremities (nose, ears, feet and tail). It will weigh about 4·1 kg. (9 lbs.) and looks like a large Himalayan.

Chinchilla
Another of the original fur breeds, it will weigh about 2·7 kg. (6 lbs.). Said to be developed as an alternative to the expensive pelt of the Chinchilla rodent, which the rabbit certainly resembles in color. A deservedly popular breed among rabbit fanciers. A larger variety – the Chinchilla Giganta is sometimes available.

Fox
In company with the Chinchilla, a fur breed. The Silver Fox has a black back, with abundant white ticking along the sides, and a white stomach. The blue and chocolate are similar but with blue and chocolate replacing the black, respectively. It will weigh about 2·7 kg. (6 lbs.).

A Silver Fox rabbit

A New Zealand White rabbit with his guinea pig friend. Both will live quite happily together.

Havana
A self-chocolate colored breed which, ideally, should be as dark as possible. It is of medium size.

Lilac
The lilac is a medium-sized, self-colored breed of a pretty, dove-gray color. It is not bred in large numbers.

New Zealand Black
A large, solidly built animal developed in the U.S.A. as a meat breed. The color is black and weight will be in the order of 4·1kg. (9lbs.).

New Zealand Red
This is a British breed and much older than its two namesakes. The color is a dark orange-red and it possesses an unusually short, harsh coat.

New Zealand White
A large breed, similar to the New Zealand Black and bred in the U.S.A. for the same purpose. The color is albino (white coat and pink eyes).

Rex
The Rex is remarkable in having a short, plush-like, coat, as if sheared. The unusual coat is due to a genetic mutation. The Rex is popular and is bred in many colors; in fact in nearly all of the possible colors. Black, blue, chocolate, lilac, white and many others. In addition to ordinary Rex, there is an interesting variation with a wavy coat known as Astrex and an extraordinary long-haired type known as Opossum Rex.

Sable
This is a fascinating blend of dark and light sepia-brown tones. The back is dark-colored, shading to lighter sepia on the sides and stomach. In the Siamese Sable, the shading continues right to the stomach but, in the Marten Sable, the shading is interrupted by white ticking and stomach as in the Fox. Weight is about 2·7kg. (6lbs.).

Satin
The outstanding feature of the Satin is the high gloss given off by the coat. All rabbits in superb condition have a glossy coat, but this cannot compare with the sheen of the Satin. The Satin occurs in a large number of color varieties which is often darkened by the action of the satinization, and they weigh about 3·2kg. (7lbs.).

Smoke Pearl
This is a shaded breed, similar to the Sable but in tones of smoky-blue and pearl-blue. The back is darkest, shading to lighter flanks and belly fur. The Smoke may be found either as Siamese or as Marten varieties, the latter having white ticking along the sides and white stomach fur. Smoke Pearls will weigh about 2·7kg. (6lbs.).

The Smoke Pearl rabbit

6. Exhibitions

Anyone who has progressed beyond the 'pet keeping' stage will soon encounter a whole new world, that of the exhibition rabbit. Rabbit shows are an annual, quarterly or monthly event in many parts of the country. Newcomers are invariably welcomed and made to feel at home. It is easy to pick up an enthusiasm for showing. The beginner is catered for by 'novice' classes from which experienced fanciers are excluded. Even if you feel your rabbits are not up to show standard, these can be entered in 'pet' classes in which entries are judged for health and condition rather than for exhibition qualities.

If you become interested in shows, it is advisable to join the local rabbit club. These cannot exist without continuing support, and membership means meeting other people who are interested in keeping rabbits as an enjoyable hobby. Many people who regularly attend shows regard these as social events, apart from the business of exhibiting. It is an opportunity to chat with like-minded people. Your local community centre ought to be able to advise on the name and address of the nearest rabbit club.

The Argenté is not popular as a pet but is a good show rabbit.

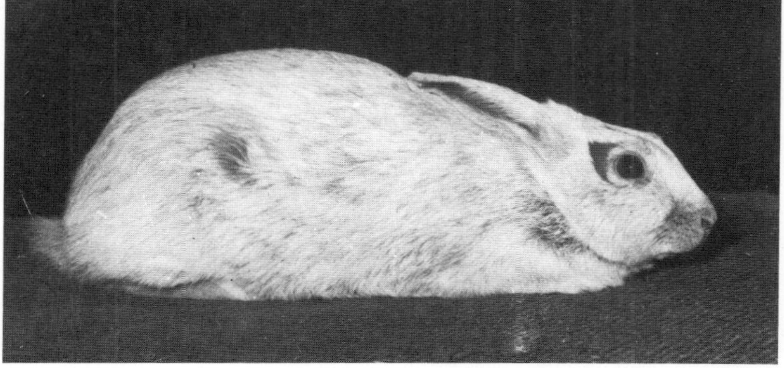

Shows

Rabbit shows are organized at several levels. The local show may take place as a community activity but larger, more specialized, shows also occur. These are arranged by societies devoted to the interest of specific breeds. The local club caters for all breeds, whereas the specialist society is concerned with only one breed. The society may cover the whole country (national club), or defined areas (regional club). If a certain breed is very popular or 'strong' numerically, both national and regional societies may exist. The really keen rabbit fancier usually joins at least his or her club and the national body of the breed(s) in which he or she is most interested.

National societies normally hold two shows per year. The first is the young stock show (the current season's breeding) and the second, the adult stock show (where adults of all ages compete). Wins at these shows carry greater prestige than those at local level. In fact, wins at these shows usually proclaim that the rabbits are the best of their breed – a very considerable honor, as competition is fierce.

There are a few do's and don'ts in exhibiting a rabbit. First of all, never take an ill animal to a show, nor one which is out of condition – where the bones can be felt by caressing the animal. It will certainly lose marks. Also, do not

The Dutch rabbit is a perennial favorite, both as a pet and an exhibition animal – as a result standards are very high and competition keen.

The beautiful Ermine Rex rabbit will need careful preparation for its show days.

take a rabbit which is obviously molting, this is considered a fault in almost all breeds. If there are slight signs of molt, try to remove them by light grooming with a clean cloth.

Any stains on the feet or stomach may be removed by sponging with a good quality soft soap and water. If you do use a white powder (on white rabbits), this must be completely removed by the day of the show. Actually the use of powder at any time is unwise and should be unnecessary if the rabbit is kept hygienically. Clipping or dyeing is illegitimate and could lead to disqualification (as well as disgrace!).

Show stock must be tractable on the judging table, for a vicious or obstreperous animal will loose marks even if it is not disqualified. It follows that show rabbits should be petted regularly so that they are used to human handling. Do not be backward in talking to the animal as you fondle and groom it so that it becomes accustomed to the human voice and the hubbub of a show. Never handle a rabbit on a smooth surface, for it will almost

The Black and Tan rabbit should have a good sheen to its coat. They are a small variety and make fine pets and show animals.

certainly skid and slide, and become alarmed. Use a bench or table upon which a sack has been carefully stretched. These may seem insignificant points, but they are part of the art of showing.

Classes

Beginners may like to know about the type of classes ('schedule') that are staged at a typical show. Pet classes for bucks, does or either sex, perhaps differentiated by age, would be for all animals, but judged largely on health. Novice classes are intended for exhibitors who have not won a first prize (or other award) before. All beginners should enter these classes because they are designed for them and they stand the best chance of winning a prize.

'Straight' classes are for particular breeds or sexes of a particular breed. The number of these will vary with the size and nature of the event. These classes are the main purpose of the show. 'Duplicate' classes are those where the different breeds compete against each other; for example, 'Best Fancy' for all fancy breeds, or 'Best Fur' for all fur breeds. There may be special category classes, such as 'breeders', where the rabbit must be bred by the exhibitor. The challenge is where all of the exhibits compete for Best in Show, a very high honor which many breeders esteem. A beginner is free to enter for any of these classes but it should be remembered that the competition will be stiff.

Prizes

Prize cards are issued to all winners. There are seven in all, in the following order of merit, First, Second, Third, Reserve, Very Highly Commended, Highly Commended, and Commended. The value of these cards will vary with the number of exhibits in the class. A Reserve in a class of forty may be more meritorious than a First in a class of four. Certain prize cards may be withheld if the judge does not consider that the exhibits are good enough.

In addition, there are often special prizes for certain breeds or breed categories, such as Best Fancy or Best Fur rabbit. There may be certificates of merit, diplomas or rosettes. Some shows are more lavish with these than others. There are more substantial prizes in the shape of silver cups, bowls, or plaques. Frequently, these latter are reserved for members only, especially if they are valuable.

Generally speaking, the entry fees are not exorbitant; conversely the prize money is not very substantial. A visit to a show should be made in the spirit

The Chinchilla rabbit

of an outing where one can admire the exhibits in friendly conversation with people who share a common interest in rabbits and everything to do with rabbits.

Travelling Boxes

If much showing is anticipated, a box for carrying the exhibits to and from the show is essential. These are called 'travelling boxes' and are made of a light-weight material, such as plywood. The box should be well ventilated and roomy enough for the rabbit to be comfortable. Large breeds will require a bigger box than small breeds. A box 25cm. (10in.) wide, 46cm. (18in.) long and 30cm. (12in.) high would be suitable for many breeds. The majority of boxes are carried by a stout leather strap fitted lengthways over the top of the box. This avoids any strain upon the lid which can be closed by simple snap fasteners. These boxes may be bought or made at home by a handyman.

Travelling box for two rabbits

Pretty pets, like this one, can be entered in special classes at shows. They do not have to be regular breeds, but must be appealing and healthy.

The Lilac rabbit is seldom kept as a pet.

7. First Aid

Stock kept under proper conditions of housing, and adequately fed, rarely fall ill. Does may become out of condition as a result of suckling a litter, but this is normal and they will recover once the litter is weaned. Unfortunately, illness can strike at any time and a brief description of the more common complaints may not be amiss.

The healthy rabbit has a well-kept appearance, is bright of eye, alert in manner and inquisitive of any movement. Contrariwise, the out-of-sorts individual often has an ill-kept coat, is dull of eye and listless in behavior. The eyes may be half, or wholly, closed. More serious, there is usually a lack of desire to eat.

The rabbit, unfortunately, appears unable to offer much resistance to disease. Prevention is better than cure, it would seem, and such measures fall under a variety of headings.

(i) Always feed a varied diet, so that if anything obnoxious is accidentally included, insufficient will be fed to be harmful. Also, any possible deficiency disease may be avoided.

(ii) Keep the hutches, feeding bowls, water bottles, hay racks and cleaning tools as clean as possible. Avoid storing food next to hutch cleanings.

(iii) Avoid over-crowding young or adults. More stock than can be tended comfortably, spells neglect and potential trouble.

(iv) Do not put youngsters from different litters in the same hutch. Although each may appear healthy, one litter may transmit a disease to the other which is harmful.

(v) Should new stock be acquired at any time, keep these separate from the other rabbits until they can be given a clean bill of health.

Diarrhea

Rabbits, especially young ones, are most susceptible to attacks of diarrhea. Alas, it is not easy to finger the cause. In the past, wet or excessively juicy green-food has been blamed for an attack. Again, green-food which has become yellow or 'over-heated' due to lying in a heap has been implicated. Moldy hay could also be a cause. In fact, any tainted food can lead to a stomach upset and diarrhea. Treatment would be to withhold green-food and feed only corn, hay and water.

A severe form of diarrhea is termed 'scours' by rabbit fanciers, and could be likened to dysentery in humans. The symptoms appear quite suddenly, with loss of appetite and condition. Death occurs within a few days. It is rarely worth trying to effect a cure. Scours should be treated as an infectious disease, and the hutch should be thoroughly scrubbed with a solution of disinfectant. All feeding bowls, water bottles and other utensils should be similarly washed. Any hay in the hutch should be burnt.

Bloat

Distention of the abdomen is the primary symptom of this disease. The contents of the abdomen often appear hard, as if the animal has constipation or the intestines are blown-up by gas. Incorrect feeding is usually blamed for the onset of bloat, although opinions differ as to the exact cause. Bloat is commonly confined to young animals and restoration to health is poor. Severe cases are best destroyed as painlessly as possible. Treat the disease as if it is infectious.

Coccidiosis

This can be a bothersome disease among young rabbits which are the most susceptible. The symptoms are not remarkable, merely loss of appetite, thinness and listlessness, often with diarrhea. The disease is due to a parasite which is passed from the mother to the young via her droppings. The young contract the disease by consuming contaminated green-food and hay. Should Coccidiosis be suspected, a veterinarian should be able to arrange a microscopic examination of the droppings (feces) for coccidia. Severe cases should be destroyed without delay, for recovery is unlikely. The hutch and utensils should be scrubbed with a strong solution of disinfectant.

Sneezing

A shake of the head, accompanied by a sneeze is common in rabbits. This is nothing more than an attempt to clear an irritant in the nostrils – a speck of dust, or a particle of hay. There may also be frequent sneezing, accompanied by a colorless discharge. This sneezing can normally also be disregarded, unless it is unusually troublesome. It is not the same as snuffles which is a more grave complaint.

Snuffles

Snuffles is not unlike sneezing initially but the discharge is white, more viscid and flows copiously. There is much pawing of the nose and the fur on the

This Flemish Giant and Netherland Dwarf are very lucky rabbits. They share a large compound to live and play in – as does the Belgian Hare. Rabbits given this sort of freedom exhibit totally different personalities to those unfortunates who are doomed to life in restricted hutches. Make sure your pet is given ample time outside of its hutch if this is not already within its own exercise area.

lower part of the front legs becomes matted. The animal may breathe noisily and the streaming nose may abate for a while but always returns. It is an infectious disease, with no known cure. The usual recommendation is for the afflicted individual to be painlessly destroyed. All bedding must be burnt and the hutch and utensils be thoroughly disinfected.

Sore Hocks

These are inflamed bare areas on the undersurface of the back legs. The Rex breed is particularly prone to this malady. It is due to rough flooring or excessively wet areas and should not arise if the flooring is made of smooth-planed timber and the hutch is kept clean. An antiseptic ointment should be smeared on the affected areas and soft hay provided for bedding. Severe cases should be referred to a veterinarian for treatment.

Wounds

The energetic rabbit may suffer from small wounds, but these normally heal themselves with little or no attention. It is advisable to clean such wounds, if dirty, and to see that inflammation does not set in. If the wound does become inflamed or fails to heal, a vet should be consulted immediately.

Weeping Eye

May arise from several causes. A common cause is foreign matter in the eye. If so, the eye should be examined and the offending matter removed (for example, a speck of hay or whatever). The eye may become red and tender, in which case an infection has occurred, and it is wise for the eye to be seen by a vet. The eye is too delicate an organ to be treated by home cures.

Vent Disease

This affliction appears as continuous ulceration of the sex organs of both sexes, the penis and surrounding skin for the male and the vent for the female. It is distinguished from a passing sore or accidental wound by its persistence. The ulceration may spread to the eyes. The disease is contageous and is passed on by the act of mating. The genitals of any rabbit should be inspected for sores before copulation is allowed, particularly those of any rabbit which is not known personally. Treatment is feasible but will necessitate a visit to a vet.

Milk Fever

Should a doe lose a litter shortly after giving birth, the milk may accumulate in the milk glands. These will become swollen, hard and obviously painful. The remedy is to mate the doe as soon as possible, the event of pregnancy helping to halt the flow of milk and relieving the pressure within the glands. Failing this veterinary advice should be sought.

Ear Infection

If the rabbit shows signs of excessive scratching of the ears or head shaking, the problem may be an infection. In bad cases, the animal may cry out with pain when the ears are touched. The infection can be seen as a brownish encrustation inside the base of the ears and is due to miscroscopic mites. Treatment consists of removal of the encrustation and insertion of a parasiticide which can be supplied by a vet. The disease is known as 'ear canker'.

Toe-nails

The nails of the front feet are rarely a problem but those of the hind feet can become excessively long and curved. This is an affliction of the older animal but can be easily treated by clipping. One must be careful not to clip too closely to the base of the nail, otherwise a blood vessel, known as the 'quick', may be severed. Should this be done accidentally, a watch must be kept that the nail does not become infected.

Teeth Malocclusion

An occasional rabbit may suffer from a jaw defect in which the four front incisor teeth are not properly aligned. This means that the teeth, which are ever-growing, are not kept short by normal wear. Eventually they protrude like elephant tusks and interfere with eating, or they may grow up, or down, through the jaws with, unless remedied, death following. They must be clipped to a more normal size.

Tapeworm Cysts

These occur as soft swellings under the skin, frequently on the shoulders or back. They are due to accumulations of clear fluid containing the white 'eggs' of a dog tapeworm. The rabbit picks up the eggs by eating green-food fouled by dogs. This is an important reason why green-food should not be gathered from areas over-run by dogs. The cysts can be easily drained by a vet. The white tapeworm eggs must be removed during this operation, otherwise the swelling will re-appear.

Parasites

Rabbits are rarely bothered by fleas or mites, especially if the animals are kept under hygienic conditions. Should either be seen or suspected, they can be controlled by regular application of insecticidal powder as sold for cats and dogs.

Coprophagy

A rabbit may be seen to eat its own droppings, a habit known as coprophagy. This is normal and does not indicate that the diet is deficient or the animal is ill. Actually, two types of pellets are voided by the rabbit; one, a hard round pellet, the other, a softer pellet containing partially digested food. It is these latter which are eaten. Green-food and hay are not quickly digested and coprophagy gives the rabbit a chance to extract the maximum nourishment.

The Orange Rex rabbit

The New Zealand Red rabbit

Friends!

A Black Rex rabbit

A large Californian rabbit with two Netherland Dwarfs – all are Himalayan marked.

The Rabbit at a Glance

Scientific Name:	*Oryctolagus cuniculus*
Weight:	1–4·1 kg. (2–9 lbs.) depending on the breed
Longevity:	10–12 years
Dental Formula:	$\frac{2\ 0\ 3\ 3}{1\ 0\ 2\ 3}$ = ½ jaw = 28 teeth
Breeding Season:	Year round; ideally spring/summer
Gestation Period:	31 days (average)
Oestrus Cycle:	None – induced by mating
Female Number of Teats:	8
Earliest recommended Breeding Age: Both Sexes:	6 months
Upper Breeding Age: Male: Female:	10 years 5 years
Litter Size (average):	5–6 (dependent upon size)
State of Young at Birth:	Eyes closed, no fur
Weaning Age:	5–6 weeks
Diet: Essential Vitamin:	Herbivorous: 'C'
Number of Varieties (Domestic):	Over 100